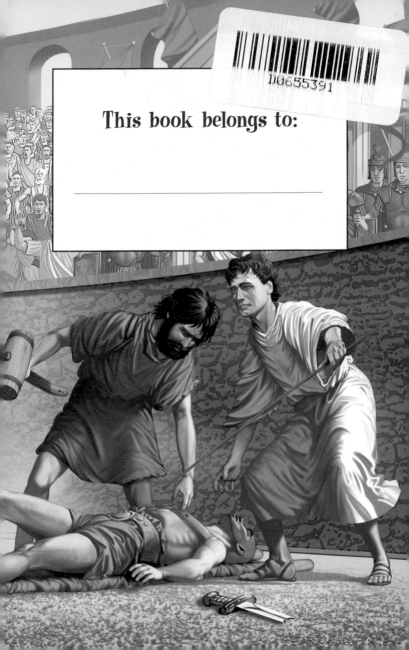

This book belongs to:

_____

Published by Ladybird Books Ltd
A Penguin Company
Penguin Books Ltd, 80 Strand, London WC2R 0RL, UK
Penguin Books Australia Ltd, Camberwell, Victoria, Australia
Penguin Books (NZ) Ltd, Cnr Airbourne and Rosedale Roads, Albany, Auckland, 1310, New Zealand

3 5 7 9 10 8 6 4 2

© LADYBIRD BOOKS MMV

Printed in Italy

Gladiators

written by Lorraine Horsley
illustrated by Laszlo Veres

Gladiators

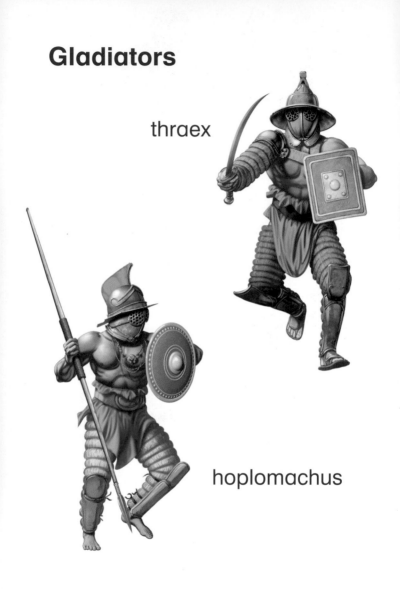

thraex

hoplomachus

retiarius

murmillo

bestiarius

7

Gladiators lived in Rome about two thousand years ago.

gladiator

9

Some gladiators were not free men. They were sold as slaves and trained to fight.

gladiator trainer

slave

Some gladiators used to fight with a net and trident.

This kind of gladiator was called a retiarius.

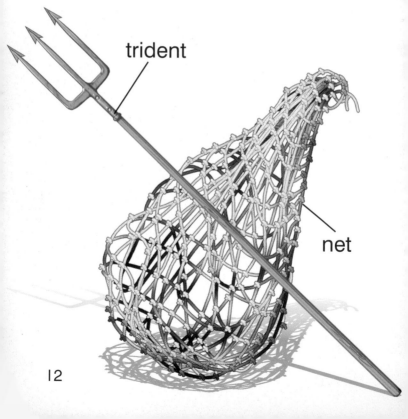

trident

net

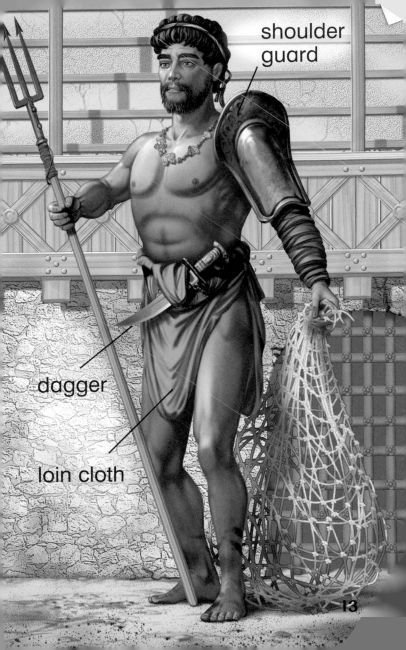

shoulder guard

dagger

loin cloth

13

Some gladiators used to fight with a curved sword.

This kind of gladiator was called a thraex.

curved
sword

helmet

small
shield

leg guard

Some gladiators used to fight with a sword and a big shield.

This kind of gladiator was called a murmillo.

sword

big shield

helmet

leg
guard

17

Some gladiators used to fight with a spear.

This kind of gladiator was called a hoplomachus.

spear

helmet

round shield

leg guard

19

Some gladiators used to fight lions or other animals.

This kind of gladiator was called a bestiarius.

21

Some gladiators lost fights.

Emperor

23

Some gladiators won fights.

bag of gold
for a prize

24

Emperor

Some gladiators won
many fights.

They were given a
wooden sword and
became free men.

wooden
sword

Glossary

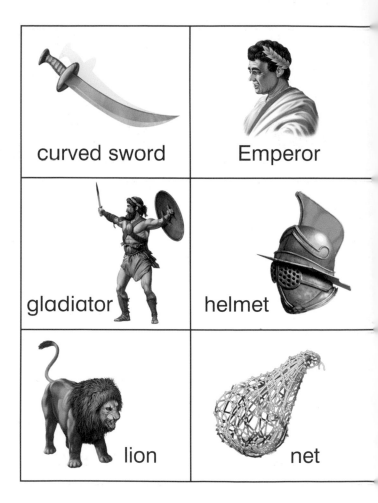

curved sword

Emperor

gladiator

helmet

lion

net

shield

slaves

spear

sword

trident

wooden sword

Index